# FABULOUS JEWELRY

## FROM
# Findings

### Chic Designs using Spacers, Caps, Clasps, and More

Mylène Hillam

*Design Originals*

an Imprint of Fox Chapel Publishing
www.d-originals.com

# Introduction

Every jewelry maker is familiar with the humble jewelry finding. They are the backbone of jewelry construction, and most of us have an assortment of them in our stash: bead caps, connectors, daisy spacers, clasps, and more. They attach components, link design elements together, and accent beads. Essentially, they are the glue that holds your jewelry together, but so often they are overlooked as nothing more than utilitarian.

But what if jewelry findings weren't just the support act? Take a closer look at the jewelry findings you have on hand. Could a bead cap become a bead? Or a lobster claw clasp a chain? Could a toggle become a decorative element?

Look closely at the jewelry in this book and you'll do a double take as you discover the designs are composed almost entirely of jewelry findings—lacy chains formed from end connectors, sculptural bracelets built using daisy spacers, and light, airy rings fashioned from hollow tubes. Styles like industrial chic, boho romantic, and sophisticated elegance can all be created solely with jewelry findings.

When you look at jewelry findings with fresh eyes, a whole new world of exciting design possibilities opens up. You now have an entirely different selection of jewelry making elements with fascinating shapes and silhouettes at your disposal. And more important, you not only have gold and silver to work with, but also a medley of antiqued and vintage finishes in a dizzying array of metallic colors.

So let's throw away any preconceived ideas of what makes a bead a bead and unlock the potential of jewelry findings—let's *make findings fabulous!*

## About the Author

Myléne Hillam (pronounced Millane) designs and creates jewelry in her studio in Brisbane, Australia. Her unique and creative designs have resulted in several significant awards, including the prized Craft and Hobby Association (CHA) Designer Press Kit Award. Her work is regularly featured in international craft publications, and she teaches and demonstrates both locally and abroad. With more than twenty years of craft experience, Myléne is passionate about passing her knowledge on to her students in her workshops.

ISBN 978-1-57421-400-0

Library of Congress Cataloging-in-Publication Data

Hillam, Myléne.
  Fabulous jewelry from findings / Myléne Hillam.
     pages cm
  Includes index.
  ISBN 978-1-57421-400-0
  1. Jewelry making. 2. Jewelry settings. I. Title.
  TT212.H55 2015
  745.594'2--dc23
              2014020221

© 2015 by Myléne Hillam and New Design Originals Corporation, *www.d-originals.com*, an imprint of Fox Chapel Publishing, 800-457-9112, 1970 Broad Street, East Petersburg, PA 17520.
Photography by Ken Bruggeman on back cover (top right) and pages 1, 2–3, 5, 6, and 7. All other project photography by Scott Kriner.

Printed in China
First printing

Acquisition editor: **Peg Couch** • Copy editor: **Colleen Dorsey**
Cover and layout designer: **Ashley Millhouse** • Editor: Katie Weeber
Photography: **Ken Bruggeman and Scott Kriner**

# Contents

# Getting Started

Before beginning the projects in this book it is helpful to have a good understanding of the techniques involved. If you're new to jewelry making, these basic techniques will help you complete the designs. Remember, as with any new skill, practice makes perfect!

## BASIC JEWELRY-MAKING TOOLS

These basic tools are everything you'll need to make the projects in this book.

Bead stoppers

Flat-nose pliers

Round-nose pliers

Chain-nose pliers

## *About Metric*

Throughout this book, you'll notice that every measurement is accompanied by a metric equivalent. Inches and feet are rounded off to the nearest half or whole centimeter unless precision is necessary. Please be aware that while this book will show 1 yard = 100 centimeters, the actual conversion is 1 yard = 90 centimeters, a difference of about 3¹⁵⁄₁₆" (10cm). Using these conversions, you will always have a little bit of extra material if measuring using the metric system.

Memory wire shears

Flush cutters

Large crimping pliers

Regular crimping pliers

Nylon jaw pliers

## OPENING AND CLOSING JUMP RINGS

## SEPARATING CHAIN LINKS

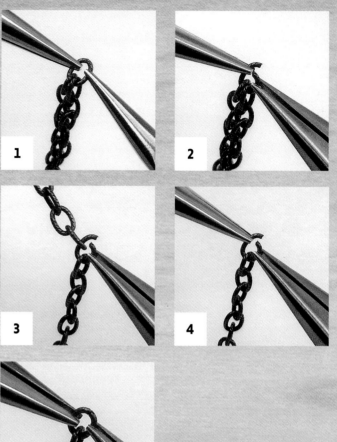

**1. Position the pliers.** Thinking of the jump ring as a clock face, position it so the opening is at twelve o'clock. With a pair of chain-nose pliers in each hand, grip the jump ring at three o'clock in your right hand and nine o'clock in your left hand.

**2. Open the jump ring.** To open the jump ring, move one hand toward you while moving the other hand away from you. Move your hands from front to back as if you are opening a door, not side to side as if you are opening a book.

**3. Check the shape.** The jump ring should look like this when opened. To close it, repeat Step 2 in reverse.

**1. Position the pliers.** Thinking of the chain link you wish to open as a clock face, position it so the opening is at twelve o'clock. With a pair of chain-nose pliers in each hand, grip the link at three o'clock in your right hand and nine o'clock in your left hand.

**2. Open the link.** Open the link just as you would open a jump ring, by moving one hand toward you while moving the other hand away from you as if you were opening a door.

**3. Remove the chain.** Remove the next link in the chain from the open link.

**4. Position the pliers.** Return the pliers to their three o'clock and nine o'clock positions.

**5. Close the link.** Repeat Step 2 in reverse to close the link. The length of chain is now ready to be used in your project.

**1. Bend the eye pin.** String a bead onto an eye pin. Then, using flat-nose pliers, bend the tail of the eye pin at a 90° angle directly above the bead.

**2. Trim the eye pin.** Trim the tail of the eye pin with flush cutters, leaving about ⅜" (1cm).

**3. Start the loop.** Place the cut end of the eye pin flush with the edge of the jaws of the round-nose pliers. Hold the pliers with your thumb facing up. Begin forming the loop by rotating your wrist inward as far as you can comfortably turn it.

**4. Complete the loop.** Remove the jaws of the pliers from the partially formed loop. Reposition the pliers so your thumb is facing up again and regrip the loop. Rotate your wrist inward as before until the loop is fully formed.

**5. Check the shape.** The simple loop should look like this.

## CREATING A WRAPPED LOOP

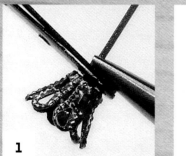

**1.** *Grip the head pin.* String the desired components onto a head pin. Then grip the head pin just above the last component added with the chain-nose pliers.

**2.** *Bend the head pin.* Bend the head pin above the jaws of the pliers at a 90° angle, creating a stem.

**3.** *Position the pliers.* Place the bottom jaw of the round-nose pliers in the bend created in Step 2.

**4.** *Start the loop.* Use your free hand to wrap the head pin wire around the top jaw of the pliers.

**5.** *Complete the loop.* Remove the jaws of the pliers from the partially formed loop. Reposition the pliers so the bottom jaw is in the partially formed loop. Use your free hand to wrap the head pin wire around the bottom jaw of the pliers to complete the loop.

**6.** *Wrap the wire.* Hold the loop flat in the jaws of flat-nose pliers. Using chain-nose pliers in your other hand, grip the end of the head pin and wrap the wire around the stem you created in Step 2 two or three times.

**7.** *Trim the wire.* Trim away the excess wire as close to the stem as you can.

**8.** *Check the shape.* The wrapped loop should look like this.

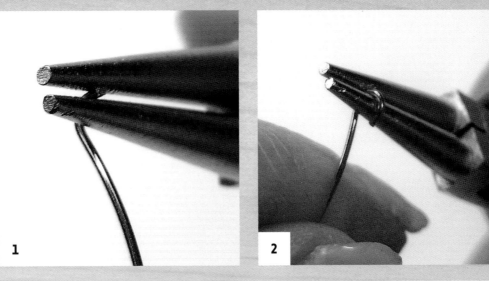

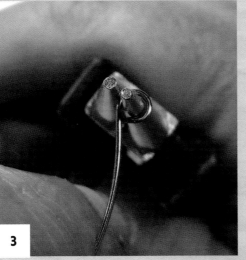

**1. *Start the loop.*** Grip the end of the memory wire with the round-nose pliers, positioning the wire so the outside curve is toward you. Make sure no wire is protruding beyond the jaws of the pliers. Holding the pliers with your thumb facing up, begin forming the loop by rotating your wrist inward as far as you can comfortably turn it.

**2. *Continue the loop.*** Remove the jaws of the pliers from the partially formed loop. Reposition the pliers so your thumb is facing up again and regrip the loop. Use your free hand to firmly push the wire against the plier jaws while rotating your wrist inward at the same time.

**3. *Complete the loop.*** Repeat Step 2 until you have a fully formed loop.

**4. *The completed end loop.*** The completed outward-facing loop should look like this. To form an inward-facing loop, form the loop on the inside curve of the memory wire instead of the outside curve.

## CRIMPING BEADING WIRE

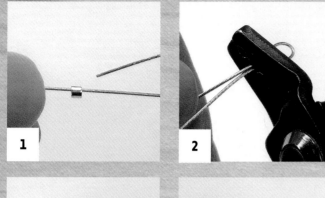

**1. String the crimp.** String the crimp onto one end of a strand of beading wire and feed the end of the wire back through the crimp, forming a loop at the end.

**2. Make the first crimp.** Place the crimp tube in the second hole of the crimping pliers (the one closest to the handles). Make sure the two strands of wire do not cross over each other and the open face of the wire loop is facing upward. Then firmly squeeze the crimp tube with the pliers to form a channel down the center of the tube with a wire strand positioned on either side.

**3. Make the second crimp.** Place the crimp tube in the first hole of the crimping pliers (farthest from the handles), positioning it so the open face of the beading wire loop sits vertically. Squeeze the crimp tube with the pliers so the spaces on either side of the channel are compressed. Tug the wire ends to make sure they are secure.

**4. Check the shape.** The crimp tube should look like this when you're finished.

## USING CRIMP COVERS

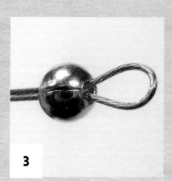

**1. Position the crimp cover.** Place the crimped tube inside the crimp cover so the crimp cover completely encloses it.

**2. Close the crimp cover.** Place the crimp cover in the first hole of the large crimping pliers (farthest from the handles). Gently squeeze the sides of the cover together to form a round bead around the crimp. Make sure the loop and wires do not get caught in the seam.

**3. Check the bead.** When finished, the crimp cover should be round and the seam should be closed as tightly as possible.

# TYING OFF ELASTIC CORD

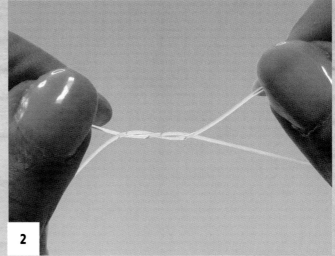

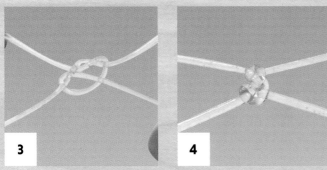

**1. Hold the elastic cord ends.** Hold one cord end in each hand and cross them over each other.

**2. Tie the first half of a square knot.** Wrap the tail of one cord around the other, creating a half knot.

**3. Tie the second half of the square knot.** Tie another half knot over the first half knot, creating a full square knot.

**4. Tighten the knot.** Pull on all strands of the elastic to tighten up the knot. Repeat Steps 1–3 to tie a second square knot, tightening the elastic after each half knot.

**5. Glue the knot.** Apply a dab of beading adhesive to the knot for added strength (I used G-S Hypo Cement).

**6. Finish off the cord.** Trim the ends to ¼" (0.5cm) and hide the cut ends inside a bead if possible.

# Bead Caps and Cones

Bead caps are some of the most decorative jewelry findings you'll have in your stash. Designed to enhance and beautify beads, they are often as important as the beads they accent. Whether you use plain metal disks, delicate filigrees, or solid cones, bead caps add substance, detail, and complexity to a jewelry design.

But what happens if you eliminate the beads from the design entirely and nest one bead cap inside another...and then layer another on top...and another? By stringing a variety of differently shaped bead caps in this manner, you can fashion ornate metal elements that will instantly transform your jewelry into treasures reminiscent of the mysterious East.

So come explore the shapes and textures of bead caps with me and let's recreate the magic and allure of the orient in *your* wardrobe.

# Oriental Gold Bracelet

Finished length: 8" (20.5cm)

## MATERIALS

- Eight 10 x 5mm gold rope bead caps
- Eight 10 x 6mm gold filigree loop bead caps
- Four 8mm clear/red-lined glass bicones
- Three 7mm gold stardust beads
- Four 5mm gold stardust beads
- Eight 3mm gold spacer beads
- 11 gold eye pins
- Gold toggle and clasp

## TOOLS

- Flat-nose pliers
- Round-nose pliers
- Flush cutters

1

2

3

4

**1. Create the bead cap eye pins.** String a 3mm spacer bead, a rope bead cap, a filigree bead cap, a glass bicone, a filigree bead cap, a rope bead cap, and a 3mm spacer bead onto an eye pin. Make sure the bead and findings are pushed firmly together. Then turn a simple loop (see page 9) close to the last spacer bead so the components will not move. Create three more eye pin beads for a total of four.

**2. Create the stardust eye pins.** String each of the stardust beads on an eye pin and turn simple loops (see page 9) at the ends.

**3. Assemble the bracelet.** Connect the eye pins by opening a loop at the end of an eye pin, putting it through a loop of another eye pin, and closing it. Use the following pattern to connect all the eye pins: two small stardust eye pins, bead cap eye pin, large stardust eye pin, bead cap eye pin, large stardust eye pin. This last eye pin is the center eye pin of the bracelet. Connect the remaining eye pins to the center eye pin in reverse order.

**4. Attach the clasp.** Open the end loop of the first and last eye pins on the bracelet, and attach one half of the clasp to each one.

Gold filigree and rope bead caps are used in conjunction to create Oriental-style focal beads for this bracelet. Pair it with a blazer for a workplace showstopper or use it to dress up your favorite t-shirt and jeans ensemble.

# Lotus Bracelet

Finished size: 2⅛" (5.5cm) internal diameter

## MATERIALS

- Two 10 x 5mm gold rope bead caps
- Two 4 x 2mm gold filigree bead caps
- Two 13 x 7mm gold 8-petal bead caps
- Six 13 x 7mm silver 8-petal bead caps
- Six 9.5 x 3mm silver star-shaped bead caps
- Six 4 x 2mm silver filigree bead caps
- Forty-eight 8 x 3mm silver rope bead caps
- Three 8mm silver filigree balls
- One 8mm gold filigree ball
- 12" (30.5cm) of 1mm beading elastic

## TOOLS

- Scissors
- Bead stopper
- Jewelry adhesive or clear nail polish (I used G-S Hypo Cement)

1

2

6

**1. Prepare the elastic.** Prepare the elastic by stretching it three or four times. Attach the bead stopper to one end.

**2. Begin the stringing pattern.** String a silver filigree ball, a silver 8-petal bead cap, a silver star-shaped bead cap, and a silver filigree bead cap onto the elastic.

**3. Form the side of the bracelet.** String twenty silver rope bead caps onto the elastic.

**4. Create a silver focal bead.** String the following silver components onto the elastic: a silver filigree bead cap, a silver

star-shaped bead cap, a silver 8-petal bead cap, a silver filigree ball, a silver 8-petal bead cap, a silver star-shaped bead cap, and a silver filigree bead cap.

**5. String the spacer bead caps.** String four silver rope bead caps onto the elastic.

**6. Create the gold focal bead.** String the following gold components onto the elastic: a gold filigree bead cap, a gold rope bead cap, a gold 8-petal bead cap, the gold filigree ball, a gold 8-petal bead cap, a gold rope bead cap, and a gold filigree bead cap. This is the center of the bracelet.

**7. Finish stringing the bracelet.** String the other side of the bracelet to match, but omit the second silver filigree focal bead at the end.

**8. Tie off the bracelet.** Tie the ends of the elastic together in a half knot. Tie a second knot, pulling on all strands of the elastic to stretch and tighten it. Tie another knot and stretch it again. Apply jewelry adhesive or nail polish to the knot and allow it to dry thoroughly. Trim the ends to ¼" (0.5cm) and hide them within the first bead cap.

Petal bead caps are used to create lotus flower focal beads. This piece can go dressy or casual depending on your outfit.

# Filigree Cluster Earrings

Finished length: 2" (5cm)

## MATERIALS

- Two 10 x 5mm gold rope bead caps
- Two 4 x 2mm gold filigree bead caps
- Two 13 x 7mm gold 8-petal bead caps
- Six 13 x 7mm silver 8-petal bead caps
- Six 9.5 x 3mm silver star-shaped bead caps
- Six 4 x 2mm silver filigree bead caps
- Forty-eight 8 x 3mm silver rope bead caps
- Three 8mm silver filigree balls
- One 8mm gold filigree ball
- 12" (30.5cm) of 1mm beading elastic

## TOOLS

- Chain-nose pliers

**2**

**3**

**4**

**1. Prepare the chain.** Separate the chain into two seven-link lengths. Set one aside. Attach one end of the remaining chain to an earring wire.

**2. Create a bead cap disk.** Place two gold bead caps together, insides facing, to create a disk shape. Thread a jump ring through one of the outer holes of each bead cap to hold them together. Use the jump ring to attach the disk to the bottom link of the chain with the earring wire attached.

**3. Begin attaching the disks.** Create another gold bead cap disk and attach it to the left side of the second from bottom link of the chain. Create a silver bead cap disk and attach it to the right side of the same link.

**4. Continue the stringing pattern.** Repeat Step 3 to attach disks to the third from bottom link of the chain. This time, attach the gold disk to the right side and the silver disk to the left side. Repeat Steps 2 and 3 to attach disks to all the remaining links of the chain, alternating the colors on each side.

**5. Make the second earring.** Repeat Steps 1–4 to make a second earring to match.

The extra small bead caps used to make these earrings create a lot of movement and a lot of sparkle—and the mix of gold and silver is right on trend.

# Layered Petals Ring  Finished size: 1¼" (3cm) diameter

## MATERIALS

- Two 17mm silver adjustable filigree leaf bead caps
- One 25mm silver water lily bead cap
- One 15 x 7.5mm silver flower bead cap
- One 12 x 8mm silver bell-shaped bead cap
- One 6 x 7mm silver cone
- 1 clear silicone earring stopper
- 3 silver chain tabs
- One 25mm silver flat filigree adjustable ring base

## TOOLS

- Chain-nose pliers
- Round-nose pliers
- Flush cutters
- Scissors

**1. Attach the head pin.** Thread the head pin through the center hole of the ring base from the back to the front.

**2. String the lower petals.** Thread the outer points of the two adjustable filigree leaf bead caps onto the head pin with the inside curve of each bead cap facing upward to form a cup shape.

**3. String the bead caps and prepare the earring stopper.** String the water lily, flower, bell, and cone bead caps onto the head pin with the inside curve of each bead cap facing up. String the earring stopper onto the head pin and push it down into the cone. Mark the area of the stopper that is visible above the cone. Remove the stopper from the head pin and trim away the marked area. String the trimmed stopper onto the head pin.

**4. Finish the ring.** Arrange the filigree leaves at the bottom of the ring evenly around the head pin. Trim the end of the head pin to ⅜" (1cm). Make sure the findings are pushed firmly together. Then turn a simple loop (see page 9) as close to the earring stopper as possible.

**5. Add the stamens.** Open the loop of the head pin, hook on the three chain tabs, and close the loop.

This ring has a classic, romantic look with lots of visual interest created by the layers of findings. Spin the petal layers around on the ring base to create the perfect look.

# Cone Drop Earrings

Finished length: 3⅛" (8cm)

## MATERIALS

- Two 11 x 9mm silver cones
- Two 10 x 7mm silver cones
- Two 7.5 x 6mm silver cones
- Two 4 x 3mm silver Bali spacer beads
- Six 3mm silver spacer beads
- Six 60mm silver head pins
- Two 6mm silver jump rings
- 2 silver earring wires

## TOOLS

- Chain-nose pliers
- Round-nose pliers
- Flush cutters

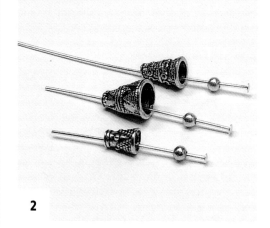

2

3

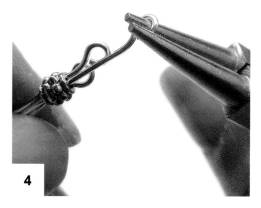

4

5

**1. Trim the head pins to size.** Trim one head pin to 1⅜" (3.5cm) and another to 1¾" (4.5cm).

**2. String the bead cones.** String a 3mm spacer bead and the smallest cone onto the shortest head pin. String a 3mm spacer bead and the largest cone onto the medium head pin. String a 3mm spacer bead and the medium cone onto a full size head pin.

**3. String the Bali spacer bead.** Place the ends of the three beaded head pins even with one another and string a Bali spacer bead onto all three together.

**4. Turn simple loops.** Turn a simple loop (see page 9) on the end of each beaded head pin.

**5. Assemble the earring.** Open a jump ring, hook on the beaded head pins and an earring wire, and close the ring.

**6. Position the Bali bead.** Slide the Bali bead up against the head pin loops and gently bend the short and long head pins slightly outward from the center of the bead to keep it in position.

**7. Make the second earring.** Repeat steps 1–6 to make a second matching earring.

Dress up a casual outfit with these flirty dangle earrings. The etched cone beads and simple curves make them the perfect accessory for a t-shirt and jeans ensemble.

# Links, Spacer Bars, and Connectors

Links, spacer bars, and connectors are a diverse group of jewelry components. With their built-in loops and holes, their function is to either connect or separate elements. Some are intricately detailed and showy, adding an element of flair to the design, while others are intentionally plain and unassuming so they can be hidden discreetly among the jewelry elements.

With so many loops and holes to work with, it is tempting to pass stringing material through each and every one. But I want to let you in on a little secret: You don't have to use every hole in a spacer bar, nor every loop of an end connector. Be selective about the loops and holes you use—offsetting some, using some more than once, and skipping others altogether. In the process, you'll transform the spacer bars and connectors into architectural building blocks. With both plain and textured surfaces to work with, you can construct jewelry like the edgy, industrial Bricks and Sticks Bracelet (page 34), the vintagey Art Deco Necklace (page 37), and the elegantly ornate Metal Lace Bracelet (page 52).

So let's transform these workhorse components into show-stopping jewelry—let's make them the stars of the show!

# Daisy Link Earrings

Finished length: 3¾" (9.5cm)

### MATERIALS

- Eight 17mm silver 5-hole daisy spacer bars
- Six 20mm silver 6-hole daisy spacer bars
- Six 13mm silver 4-hole daisy spacer bars
- Six 8mm gold daisy spacers
- Twenty-six 5 x 3mm silver oval jump rings
- Six 4mm silver jump rings
- Two 6mm silver jump rings
- 2 silver earring wires

### TOOLS

- Chain-nose pliers

1

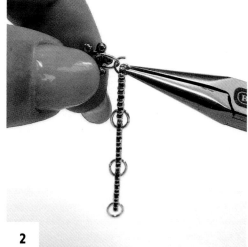

2

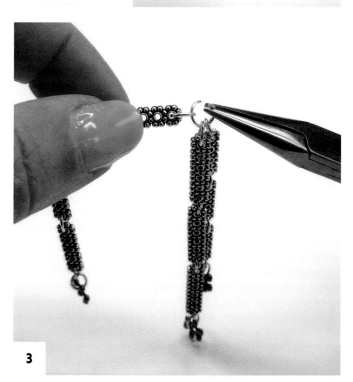

3

**1. Create the dangles.** Connect four 5-hole daisy spacer bars together, end to end, using oval jump rings. Repeat to connect three 6-hole spacer bars end to end. Finally, connect three 4-hole spacer bars together end to end.

**2. Add the accent daisies.** Open three oval jump rings and hook a gold daisy spacer onto each one before closing. Attach one of these to one end of each of the three spacer bar dangles from Step 1 using a 4mm jump ring. Attach an oval jump ring to the other end of each spacer bar dangle.

**3. Assemble the earrings.** Open a 6mm jump ring and hook on the three dangles from shortest to longest using the oval jump rings at the end of each dangle. Attach the earring wire before closing the jump ring.

**4. Make the second earring.** Repeat Steps 1–3 to make a second matching earring.

Linked spacer bars are used to create sleek chains that will dance around your shoulders. The added gold daisy spacers give the ends of the earrings a pop of color.

# Diamond Spacer Earrings

Finished length: 1½" (4cm)

## MATERIALS
- Eight 12mm gold 4-hole wave spacers
- Twelve 4mm gold jump rings
- 2 gold earring wires

## TOOLS
- Chain-nose pliers

**1.** *Connect the first set of spacers.* Place two spacers alongside each other and attach them at the second and fourth holes using jump rings.

**2.** *Connect the second set of spacers.* Repeat Step 1 with two additional spacers.

**3.** *Connect the spacer sets.* Place the two spacer sets alongside each other and attach them at the first and third holes using jump rings.

**4.** *Attach the earring wire.* Open the loop of an earring wire and hook it through the end hole of one of the outer spacers.

**5.** *Make the second earring.* Repeat Steps 1–4 to make a second matching earring.

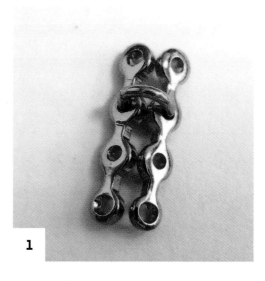

1

3

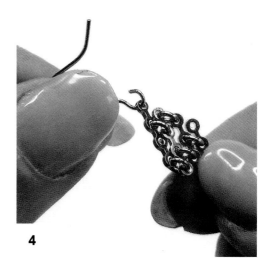

4

These earrings have such a classic look, it's hard to believe they are made using only findings! Pair these with a formal dress for an elegant evening or use them to add some sophisticated style to a more casual outfit.

# Gold and Silver Spacer Ring

Finished size: ¾" (2cm) internal diameter

## MATERIALS

- Eleven 12mm gold 4-hole wave spacers
- Eleven 12mm silver 4-hole wave spacers
- Forty-four 4mm gold jump rings

## TOOLS

- Chain-nose pliers

**1**

**2**

**1.** *Connect the first two spacers.* Place a gold and a silver spacer alongside each other and attach them at the second and fourth holes using jump rings.

**2.** *Add a third spacer.* Place a gold spacer alongside the silver spacer from the set you created in Step 1. Attach them at the first and third holes using jump rings.

**3.** *Continue the pattern.* Continue adding silver and gold spacers, using alternating holes to attach them, until all the spacers have been added.

**4.** *Complete the ring.* Connect the first and last spacers to form the ring.

**4**

This lacy ring is soft and fluid, making it extra comfortable to wear. It's simple and subtle, so you can easily pair it with just about anything.

# Bricks and Sticks Bracelet

Finished length: 7⅝" (19.5cm)

## MATERIALS

- Twenty 17 x 3.5mm gold 3-hole flat spacer bars
- Twenty 17 x 3.5mm silver 3-hole flat spacer bars
- Twenty 17 x 3.5mm brass 3-hole flat spacer bars
- Thirty-two 17 x 3.5mm gunmetal 3-hole flat spacer bars
- 8 copper eye pins
- Sixteen 4mm silver jump rings
- Three 6mm silver jump rings
- 1 silver magnetic clasp

## TOOLS

- Chain-nose pliers
- Round-nose pliers
- Flush cutters

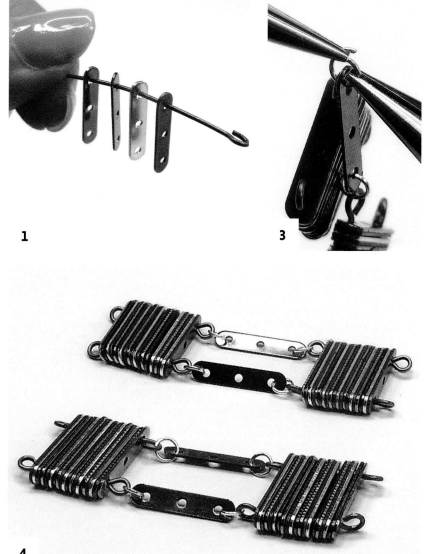

**1.** *Create the first brick.* Using the first hole of each spacer bar, string twenty spacers onto an eye pin. Use the following pattern: brass, silver, gunmetal, and gold. Turn a simple loop (see page 9) at the end of the eye pin.

**2.** *Insert a second eye pin.* Thread a second eye pin through the third hole of each of the twenty spacers from Step 1. Turn a simple loop (see page 9) at the end of the eye pin. Repeat Steps 1–2 to create three more bricks for a total of four.

**3.** *Connect two bricks.* Place two bricks end to end with the eye pins positioned vertically. Attach a 4mm jump ring to each end of a gunmetal spacer bar. Using the jump rings, attach one end of the gunmetal spacer bar to the bottom left loop of the top brick and the other end to the top left loop of the bottom brick. Repeat on the right side of the bricks with another gunmetal spacer.

**4.** *Connect the remaining bricks.* Repeat Step 3 with the two remaining bricks. When finished, you will have a pair of connected bricks.

If you like industrial chic style, with lots of mixed metals, this bracelet is for you! Pair it with the Industrial Chic Necklace and Earrings on page 46.

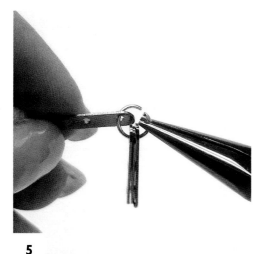

**5**

**6**

**8**

**5. *Create the crossbar.*** Open a 6mm jump ring and hook on four gunmetal spacer bars using the first hole of each spacer.

**6. *Attach the crossbar.*** Attach a 4mm jump ring to the third hole of each spacer in the crossbar. With the 6mm jump ring in the center, position the spacers of the crossbar to form an X. Place the connected bricks from Step 4 on either side of the crossbar as shown. Connect the crossbar to the loops of the bricks using the jump rings.

**7. *Create the bracelet ends.*** Open a 6mm jump ring and hook on two gunmetal spacer bars using the first hole of each spacer. Repeat with a second jump ring and the remaining two spacer bars.

**8. *Attach the bracelet ends.*** Use 4mm jump rings to attach the bracelet ends to the eye pin loops at each end of the bracelet.

**9. *Complete the bracelet.*** Attach one half of the clasp to the 6mm jump rings at each end of the bracelet.

# Art Deco Necklace

Finished size: 16" (40.5cm) internal diameter

## MATERIALS

- Twenty-four 13mm silver 4-hole daisy spacer bars
- Sixteen 17mm silver 5-hole daisy spacer bars
- Thirteen 20mm silver 6-hole daisy spacer bars
- Forty-eight 7.5mm gold daisy spacers
- Forty-six 7.5mm silver daisy spacers
- Fourteen 6 x 4mm silver oval jump rings
- 2 silver wire guardians
- 2 size 2 silver crimp tubes
- 12" (30.5cm) of 0.015", 19-strand silver beading wire
- 1 silver lobster claw clasp

## TOOLS

- Chain-nose pliers
- Flush cutters
- Crimping pliers

This bold geometric design makes a beautiful statement piece to jazz up any outfit.

**1**

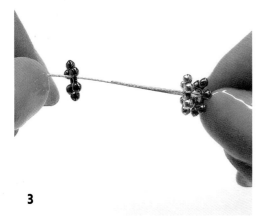

**3**

**4**

**1. *Create the spacer bar chains.*** Connect six 4-hole daisy spacer bars together, end to end, using jump rings. Attach a jump ring to each end of the spacer bar chain. Repeat to create a second spacer bar chain with a jump ring at each end.

**2. *Crimp the wire end.*** String a crimp tube and a wire guardian onto one end of the beading wire, threading the wire through both holes of the wire guardian. Bring the tail end of the beading wire back through the crimp tube and crimp securely.

**3. *String the daisy spacers.*** Alternate stringing gold and silver daisy spacers onto the wire until twenty-four gold and twenty-three silver spacers have been added. Start and end with a gold spacer.

**4. *String the 4-hole spacers.*** String a 4-hole spacer bar onto the beading wire using the first hole of the spacer. String on another 4-hole spacer bar using the second hole. Repeat until a total of six 4-hole daisy spacer bars have been added.

**5. *String the 5-hole spacers.*** String eight 5-hole spacer bars onto the wire in the following manner: first hole, second hole, third hole, second hole, first hole, second hole, third hole, and second hole.

**6. *String the 6-hole spacers.*** String twelve 6-hole spacer bars, repeating the following pattern: first hole, second hole, third hole, second hole. Finish the pattern by adding one more spacer bar using the first hole, for a total of thirteen 6-hole spacer bars.

**7. *Complete the stringing pattern.*** Repeat steps 5 and 4 in reverse to match the other side of the necklace. Repeat Step 3.

**8. *Crimp the findings in place.*** String a crimp tube and a wire guardian onto the wire, threading the wire through both holes of the wire guardian. Bring the tail end of the wire back through the crimp tube and the first few daisy spacers. Make sure the findings are pushed firmly together and crimp securely. Trim away the excess wire.

**9. *Finish the necklace.*** Connect the daisy spacer bar chains created in Step 1 to each end of the necklace. Attach the lobster claw clasp to one end.

# Waterfall Earrings

Finished length: 4¾" (12cm)

## MATERIALS

- Forty-four 15mm silver twisted curved 2-hole links
- Sixteen 4 x 5mm copper spacer beads
- Two 27mm silver 2-hole end connectors
- 4 silver eye pins
- Thirty-two 4mm silver jump rings
- 2 silver earring wires

## TOOLS

- Chain-nose pliers
- Round-nose pliers
- Flush cutters

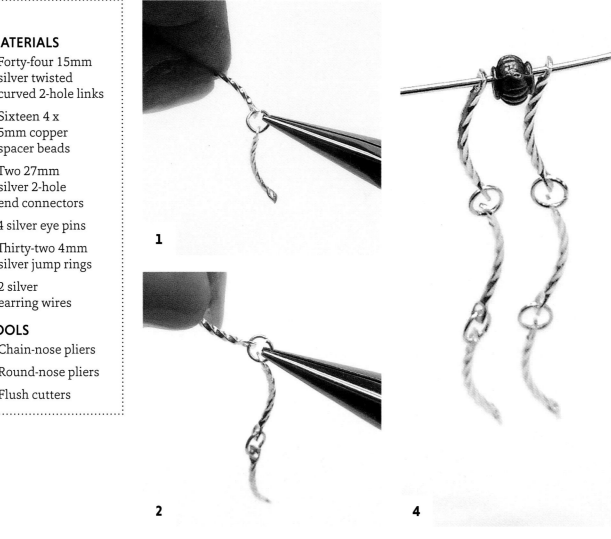

**1**

**2**

**4**

**1.** *Begin creating the wave links.* Use a jump ring to connect two curved links together with the inside curve of each link facing in opposite directions.

**2.** *Complete the wave links.* Attach another jump ring to the bottom hole of the second link and add a third link facing the opposite direction of the second link. Repeat to create five more wave links for a total of six.

**3.** *Create the short wave links.* Repeat step 1 to create two short wave links.

**4.** *Begin assembling the waterfall.* String a wave link onto an eye pin. Then, string on a copper bead and another wave link. Make sure the inside curves of the wave links are facing in the same direction. String three more copper beads, alternating them with three more wave links. You will have five wave links and four copper beads strung on the eye pin when finished. Turn a simple loop (see page 9) at the end of the eye pin.

These earrings have a beautiful fluid design with added visual interest created by the floral links and copper beads.

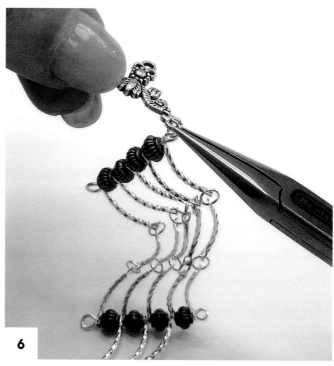

**5. *Form the second row.*** Insert a second eye pin through the bottom hole of the first wave link. String on a copper bead and then the bottom hole of the second wave link. String on one of the short wave links created in Step 3, making sure it continues the wave pattern of the second wave link. String on a copper bead, the bottom hole of the third wave link, and a long wave link. Repeat the pattern until the bottom hole of the fifth wave link has been threaded onto the eye pin. Turn a simple loop (see page 9) at the end of the eye pin.

**6. *Assemble the earring.*** Attach the loops of the top eye pin to the loops in the 2-hole end connector with jump rings. Attach the end connector to an earring wire.

**7. *Make the second earring.*** Repeat steps 1–6 to make a second matching earring.

# Lacy Birdcage Necklace

Finished length: 16½" (42cm), 4¾" (12cm) birdcage

## MATERIALS

- Twenty-four 18mm brass 3-hole end connectors
- Four 13mm antiqued copper 3-hole end connectors
- Six 14mm antiqued copper textured hollow tubes
- 6 antiqued copper eye pins
- Four 4mm antiqued copper jump rings
- Twenty-five 4mm brass jump rings
- One 8mm brass jump ring
- 1 brass lobster claw clasp

## TOOLS

- Chain-nose pliers
- Round-nose pliers
- Flush cutters

This piece has a hint of Steampunk styling, using lacy end connectors in antiqued metal colors.

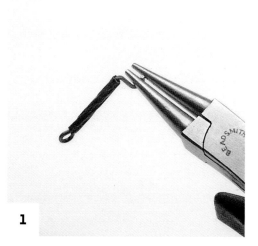

**1**

**2**

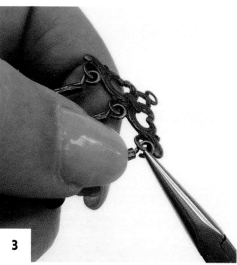

**3**

**4**

**1. *Create the birdcage bars.*** String a copper tube onto each of the eye pins and turn simple loops (see page 9) at the ends.

**2. *Attach the roof.*** Open the loop on one end of a birdcage bar and hook it through a loop of a copper end connector. Repeat to attach birdcage bars to the remaining loops of the connector.

**3. *Attach the bottom.*** Attach a second end connector to the other end of the birdcage bars. Repeat Steps 2–3 to create a second birdcage component using the remaining birdcage bars and copper end connectors.

**4. *Attach the brass connectors.*** Using an antiqued copper jump ring, attach one of the birdcage components to the first hole of a brass end connector. Attach the remaining birdcage component to the third hole of the same brass connector. The two birdcage components will be attached to one brass connector. Repeat to attach a brass connector to the bottom of both birdcage components.

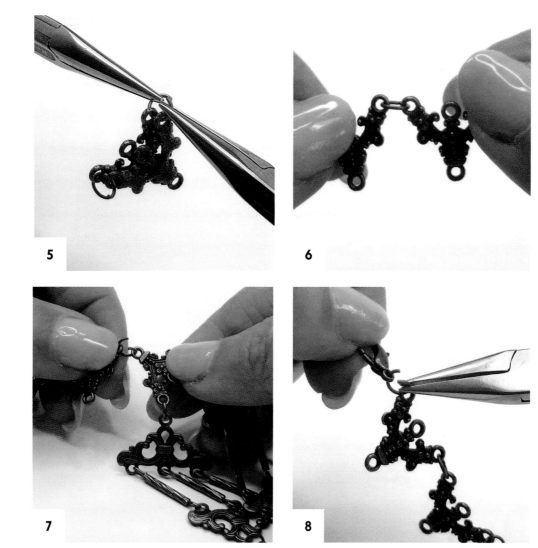

**5. Complete the birdcage.** Place two brass connectors on top of each other, right sides facing. Insert a brass jump ring through the first and third holes of both connectors to join them together. Lay the joined connectors flat and use a jump ring to attach the top hole of one connector to the bottom hole of the birdcage component.

**6. Create the lacy chain.** Attach two brass end connectors end to end by inserting a jump ring through the left hole of one and the right hole of the other. Add another connector in the same way. Continue adding connectors until you have a chain of ten. Create a second chain in the same way.

**7. Connect the birdcage to the chain.** Use a brass jump ring to attach one of the chains from Step 6 to the top hole of the birdcage component. Use a second jump ring to attach the remaining chain to the top hole of the birdcage as well.

**8. Complete the necklace.** Attach a brass jump ring to the end of each chain. Add the lobster claw clasp to one end and the 8mm jump ring to the other.

# Industrial Chic Necklace and Earrings

Finished length: 19¼" (49cm) necklace, 2" (5cm) earrings

## MATERIALS

- Eighteen 17mm gunmetal 3-hole spacer bars
- Nine 7 x 5mm gold filigree basket bead caps
- One 13 x 8mm gold filigree basket bead cap
- One 6mm gold filigree bead
- One 6mm gold fluted bead cap
- Nine 3mm gold spacer beads
- 10 gunmetal head pins
- Nineteen 4mm gunmetal jump rings
- One 6mm gunmetal jump ring
- 18½" (47cm) of 5 x 3mm gunmetal curb chain (for necklace)
- 2" (5cm) of 3 x 2mm gunmetal cable chain (for earrings)
- 1 gunmetal lobster claw clasp
- 2 gunmetal earring wires

## TOOLS

- Chain-nose pliers
- Round-nose pliers
- Flush cutters

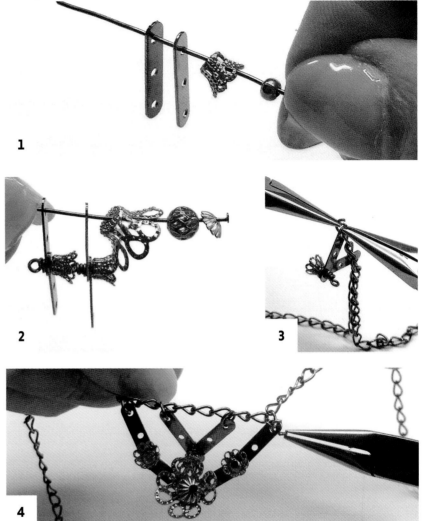

**1. Create the small daisy components.** String a 3mm bead, a small filigree bead cap, and the first holes of two 3-hole spacer bars onto a head pin. Turn a wrapped loop (see page 10) behind the spacer bar so the findings are pushed firmly together. To do this, push the components firmly down to the end of the head pin and place the jaws of the flat-nose pliers flush against the back of the last spacer bar (the thickness of the plier jaws will create a stem for wrapping the loop). Repeat to create eight more small daisy components for a total of nine components. Set two of these aside for the earrings (see Step 2 on page 48).

**2. Create the focal piece.** String the fluted bead cap, 6mm filigree bead, and large filigree basket bead cap onto a head pin. Add two of the small daisy components from Step 1, stringing them onto the head pin using the outside hole of one of the spacer bars. Note that the other spacer bar of the daisy component will hang down from the wrapped loop. Create a wrapped loop (see page 10) behind the spacer bar of the last daisy component.

**3. Begin attaching the components.** Find the center of the chain and count two links from the center link on either side. Using jump rings, attach each end of a small daisy component to these links, causing the component to form a V shape.

**4. Attach the center focal piece.** Count two links to either side of the links from Step 3 and attach each end of the focal piece to these links using jump rings, forming the focal piece into a V shape.

This ensemble combines the hard straight lines of gunmetal spacer bars with lacy gold filigree bead caps to create a unique look that's right on trend.

## FOR THE NECKLACE (CONTINUED):

**5. _Add the next daisy component._** Count two links to the right of the right focal piece link from Step 4. Using a jump ring, attach one end of a daisy component to this link. Count four links to the right of this link and attach the other end of the daisy component you just added using a jump ring.

**6. _Add the last daisy component._** Attach one end of a daisy component to the next link to the right. Count four links to the right and attach the other end of the component with a jump ring.

**7. _Complete the necklace._** Repeat Steps 5 and 6 on the left side of the necklace to match.

**8. _Attach the clasp._** Using a jump ring, attach a lobster claw clasp to one end of the necklace. Attach the 6mm jump ring to the other end.

## FOR THE EARRINGS:

1                                   2

**1. _Connect the chain to the earring wire._** Separate the chain into two 1" (2.5cm) lengths. Open a jump ring and hook on the center link of one of the chains and the loop of an earring wire.

**2. _Attach the daisy component._** Attach a jump ring to each end of the chain, and hook each end of a daisy component from Step 1 of the necklace onto each jump ring before closing them. Make sure the daisy faces front and the component forms a V shape before closing the jump rings.

**3. _Make the second earring._** Repeat Steps 1–2 to make a second matching earring.

# Silver Snowflake Choker

Finished length: 17" (43cm)

## MATERIALS

- Thirty-seven 13mm silver 3-hole rosary-style connectors
- 9" (23cm) of 6 x 4mm silver flat oval chain
- Sixty-seven 4mm silver jump rings
- Seven 6 x 4mm silver oval jump rings
- One 6mm silver jump ring
- 1 silver lobster claw clasp

## TOOLS

- Chain-nose pliers

This elegant choker combines chain with rosary-style connectors for an interesting, yet classic design. Pair it with any of the outfits in your closet—even your summer dresses!

**1. Join the connectors.** Place two connectors on top of each other, right sides facing. Insert a 4mm jump ring through the top loops of both connectors to join them together. Lay the joined connectors flat and place another connector on top of one of them. Insert another jump ring through the top loops of both stacked connectors to join them together. Continue adding connectors in this manner until you have joined seven together.

**2. Form a ring.** Use a 4mm jump ring to connect the top loops of the first and last connectors in the chain, forming a ring. This is the snowflake focal piece.

**3. Connect the outer loops.** Lay the snowflake flat and connect all the adjacent outer loops of the connectors with oval jump rings.

**4. Create the first connector chain.** Place five connectors side by side, turning the second and fourth ones upside down. Attach the connectors by using jump rings to join the adjacent loops along the top and bottom.

**5. Add two connectors.** Add two more connectors to the right end of the chain, making sure they face the same way as the end connector (all the tops and bottoms aligned). Attach them at the top and bottom using 4mm jump rings. Repeat Steps 4–5 to create a second matching chain.

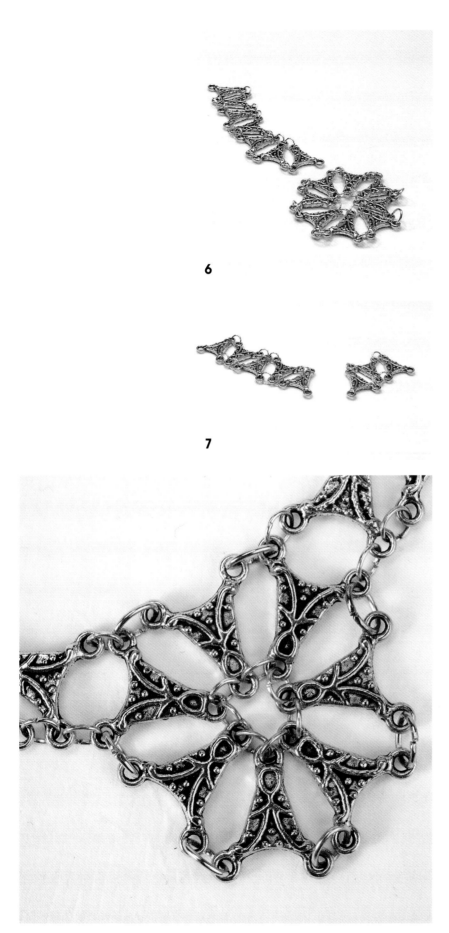

**6**

**7**

**6.** *Connect the chain to the snowflake.* Use 4mm jump rings to connect the bottom two loops of the last connector added to the chain to the bottom two loops of one of the connectors in the snowflake. Count two connectors to the right in the snowflake and connect the bottom two loops of the last connector added to the second chain to this connector. When finished, both connector chains should be attached to the snowflake and mirror one another.

**7.** *Create two additional connector chains.* Lay five connectors side by side as in Step 4 and join them together. Lay three connectors side by side as in Step 4 and join them together. Place the two lengths next to each other with the tops together and the bottoms together and connect them with jump rings. Repeat to create a matching chain of connectors.

**8.** *Begin to assemble the necklace.* Separate the chain into two 2⅛" (5.5cm) lengths and two 2⅜" (6cm) lengths. Attach jump rings to one end of all four chains. Attach the two shorter chains to the outside holes of the last end connectors attached to the snowflake section of the necklace. Attach the two longer chains to the inside holes.

**9.** *Connect the chains to the necklace.* Open the last link of each of the four chains and connect them to the last connectors added to the chain lengths created in Step 7.

**10.** *Attach the clasp.* Attach the 6mm jump ring to the outside hole of the connector at one end of the necklace and the lobster claw clasp to the outside hole of the connector at the other end.

# Metal Lace Bracelet

Finished length: 8½" (21.5cm)

**MATERIALS**
- Twenty-eight 13 x 13mm fancy gold square 4-loop connectors
- Seventy-four 4mm gold jump rings
- Gold toggle clasp

**TOOLS**
- Chain-nose pliers

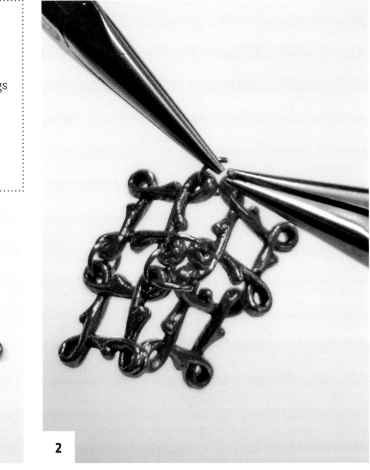

**1**                    **2**

**1. *Begin making the diamond.*** Lay four connectors out in a diamond shape. Use four jump rings to connect the four loops at the center of the diamond. Attach the left connector to the top connecter; the top connector to the right connector; the right connector to the bottom connector; and the bottom connector to the left connector.

**2. *Connect the outer loops.*** Complete the diamond by connecting each adjacent outside loop of the connectors using jump rings. When finished, you will have a loop at each point of the diamond without a jump ring attached.

**3. *Begin the second diamond.*** Use the bottom connector of the first diamond as the top connector of the second diamond. Attach three connectors to it as described in Steps 1–2 to make the second diamond.

**4. *Continue the pattern.*** Continue making diamonds until you have created nine total.

**5. *Attach the clasp.*** Add a jump ring to each end of the bracelet and attach one half of the clasp to each jump ring.

## *Tip*

To make a longer or shorter bracelet, add or remove sets of three connectors.

Gold connectors are combined in a series of diamond shapes to create this fashion-forward bracelet that's high on style, yet easy to make.

# Daisy Spacers

Daisy spacers are indispensable in building jewelry designs. These simple little flower-shaped spacers are the perfect foil to accent crystal and pearl jewelry, and they add a polished look to your jewelry designs.

But of course, there's more to daisy spacers than their ability to highlight beads. Strung en-masse, they take on a life and personality of their own. We'll be utilizing the multitude of sizes available to create eye-catching jewelry where one focal element flows into the next, almost like liquid metal ebbing and flowing. We'll build olive-shaped beads where the end of one bead becomes the beginning of the next; we'll string interlocking daisy spacers to create a modern, chunky tube-bead look; and we'll create a carved-looking sculptural bracelet. So let's get cracking and string, string, string!

# Shadows Ring

Finished size: 11⁄16" (18mm) diameter at widest point

## MATERIALS

- One hundred and eight 3mm bright silver daisy spacers
- Four 4mm bright silver daisy spacers
- Four 5mm bright silver daisy spacers
- Four 5.5mm silver daisy spacers
- Four 6mm silver daisy spacers
- Five 7mm silver daisy spacers
- Silver ring-size memory wire (25mm diameter)

## TOOLS

- Chain-nose pliers
- Memory wire shears

## Tip

To make stringing the spacers easier, hold the memory wire with the thumb and index finger of your non-dominant hand with the cut end facing up. Use your thumb to separate the coils of wire. This leaves your other hand free to thread on several spacers at a time before you need to slide them along the wire.

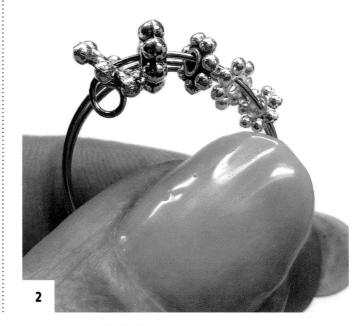

2

5

**1. Cut the ring and turn a loop.** Cut three coils from the memory wire and turn an inward facing loop (see page 11) at one end.

**2. Begin stringing the spacers.** String on a 7mm, 6mm, and 5.5mm silver daisy spacer. Then string on a 5mm and a 4mm bright silver daisy spacer.

**3. Continue stringing the ring.** String half of the 3mm bright silver daisy spacers onto the ring.

**4. String the center focal section.** String on a 4mm and a 5mm bright silver daisy spacer and then a 5.5mm, 6mm, and three 7mm silver spacers. The second 7mm spacer is the center of the ring. String the other side of the ring in reverse to match the first half.

**5. Finish the ring.** Make sure the spacers are pushed firmly together against the loop at the end of the wire. Trim the end of the wire to 3⁄8" (1cm) and turn an inward facing loop (see page 11).

Using a mix of standard and bright silver allows this ring to play with light and shadow. Pair it with the Shadows Earrings on page 58 and the Shadows bracelet on page 60.

# Shadows Earrings
Finished length: 1½" (4cm)

## MATERIALS
- Twelve 3mm bright silver daisy spacers
- Four 4mm bright silver daisy spacers
- Four 5mm bright silver daisy spacers
- Four 5.5mm silver daisy spacers
- Four 6mm silver daisy spacers
- Six 7mm silver daisy spacers
- 2 silver ball head pins
- 2 interchangeable silver earring wires

## TOOLS
- Chain-nose pliers
- Round-nose pliers
- Flush cutters

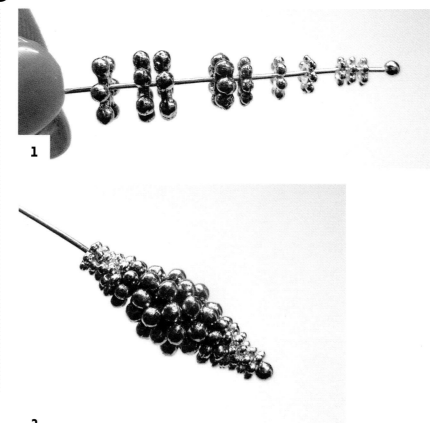

**1**

**2**

**1. *String the daisy spacers.*** String three 3mm, one 4mm, and one 5mm bright silver daisy spacer onto a head pin. Then string on one 5.5mm, one 6mm, and three 7mm silver spacers. The second 7mm spacer is the center point of the earring.

**2. *Complete the stringing pattern.*** String the second half of the earring in reverse to match the first half.

**3. *Complete the earring.*** Make sure all the spacers are pushed firmly together. Then, create a wrapped loop (see page 10) after the last daisy spacer. Slip the loop onto the earring wire and gently close the hook.

**4. *Make the second earring.*** Repeat Steps 1–3 to make a second matching earring.

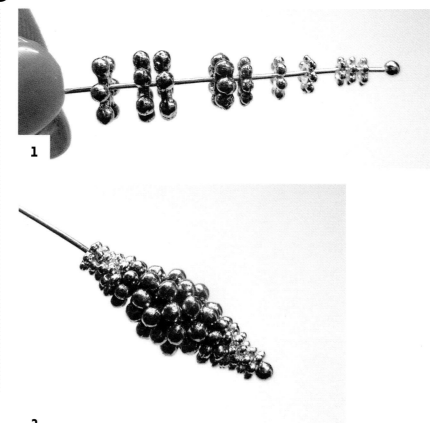

**3**

Spacers come in a vast array of sizes, so you can piece them together in various ways to create bead-like shapes, as with these earrings or the bracelet on page 60.

# Shadows Bracelet

Finished size: 2" (5cm) internal diameter

## MATERIALS

- Thirty 3mm bright silver daisy spacers
- Twenty 4mm bright silver daisy spacers
- Twenty 5mm bright silver daisy spacers
- Twenty 5.5mm silver daisy spacers
- Twenty 6mm silver daisy spacers
- Thirty 7mm silver daisy spacers
- 12" (30cm) of beading elastic
- Jewelry adhesive or clear nail polish (I used G-S Hypo Cement)

## TOOLS

- Scissors
- 1 bead stopper

2

3

**1. Prepare the elastic.** Prepare the elastic by stretching it two or three times. Attach the bead stopper to one end.

**2. Begin the stringing pattern.** String one 7mm, one 6mm, and one 5.5mm silver daisy spacer onto the elastic. Then string on one 5mm, one 4mm, and two 3mm bright silver spacers.

**3. Create the first bead.** First, string one 3mm, one 4mm, and one 5mm bright silver spacer onto the elastic. Then string on one 5.5mm, one 6mm, and three 7mm silver spacers. Finally, string on a 6mm and a 5.5mm silver spacer and one 5mm, one 4mm, and one 3mm bright silver spacer.

**4. Add a spacer.** String on one 3mm spacer.

**5. Continue the stringing pattern.** Repeat Steps 3 and 4 eight times for a total of nine beads.

**6. Complete the stringing pattern.** Repeat the stringing pattern from Step 2 in reverse to finish the half bead at the beginning of the bracelet. This means there will be ten full beads when the bracelet is tied together.

**7. Tie off the bracelet.** Tie the ends of the elastic together in a half knot. Tie a second knot, pulling on all strands of the elastic to stretch and tighten it. Tie another knot and stretch it again. Apply jewelry adhesive or nail polish to the knot and allow it to dry thoroughly.

**8. Trim the ends.** Trim the ends to ¼" (0.5cm) and thread them through the spacers to hide them.

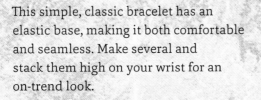

This simple, classic bracelet has an
elastic base, making it both comfortable
and seamless. Make several and
stack them high on your wrist for an
on-trend look.

# Dots and Dashes Bracelet
Finished size: 2⅛" (5.5cm) internal diameter

## MATERIALS
- Seventeen 25 x 1.5mm gold hollow spiral tubes
- 7 gold 3-hole spacer bars
- Six 3.5 x 2mm gold daisy spacers
- Eight 4 x 1mm gold daisy spacers
- Eight 4.5 x 1mm gold daisy spacers
- Eight 5 x 1mm gold daisy spacers
- Eight 6 x 1mm gold daisy spacers
- Eight 7 x 1mm gold daisy spacers
- Eight 7.5 x 1mm gold daisy spacers
- Six 8 x 1mm gold daisy spacers
- 36" (90cm) of 1.5mm beading elastic
- Jewelry adhesive or clear nail polish (I used G-S Hypo Cement)

## TOOLS
- Scissors
- 3 bead stoppers

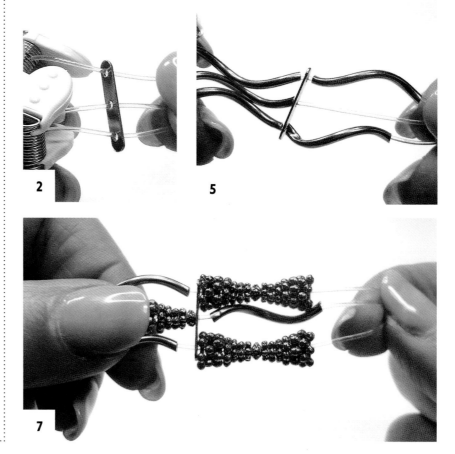

**1. Prepare the elastic.** Cut the beading elastic into three 12" (30cm) lengths. Attach a bead stopper to one end of each length.

**2. Separate the cords with a spacer bar.** Thread each of the three cords through a hole in a spacer bar.

**3. String the first section.** String a hollow tube onto each cord.

**4. String a spacer bar.** Thread each of the three cords through the corresponding holes of another spacer bar.

**5. String the second section.** String a hollow tube onto the top and bottom cords. On the middle cord, string daisy spacers in the following order: one 3.5mm, one 4mm, one 4.5mm, one 5mm, one 6mm, one 7mm, one 7.5mm, and one 8mm. Then string on one 7.5mm, one 7mm, one 6mm, one 5mm, one 4.5mm, one 4mm, and one 3.5mm daisy spacer.

**6. String a spacer bar.** Thread each of the three cords through the corresponding holes of another spacer bar.

**7. String the center section.** String a hollow tube onto the middle cord. On the top and bottom cords, string daisy spacers in the following order: one 8mm, one 7.5mm, one 7mm, one 6mm, one 5mm, one 4.5mm, one 4mm, and one 3.5mm. Then string on one 4mm, one 4.5mm, one 5mm, one 6mm, one 7mm, one 7.5mm, and one 8mm daisy spacer.

**8. String a spacer bar.** Thread each of the three cords through the corresponding holes of another spacer bar.

**9. String the fourth section.** Repeat Step 5.

**10. Complete stringing the bracelet.** Repeat Steps 2 and 3 three times.

**11. Finish the bracelet.** Working one cord at a time, tie off the end and apply a dab of adhesive to secure the knot. When the adhesive is dry, trim the end to ¼" (0.5cm) and tuck the knot and end into the bracelet to hide them.

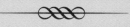

This elegant bracelet combines the smooth flowing lines of hollow tubes with textured groupings of daisy spacers to create a truly unique piece.

# Daisy Chain Choker   Finished size: 5½" (14cm)

## MATERIALS

- Seventy-three 8mm gold interlocking snowflake daisy spacers
- Eleven 15mm silver twisted curved 2-hole links
- Twenty-two 4mm silver jump rings
- Twenty 5mm gold jump rings
- Six 6mm gold jump rings
- 16" (40.5cm) of 1mm gold neck wire with threaded ball screw

## TOOLS

- Chain-nose pliers

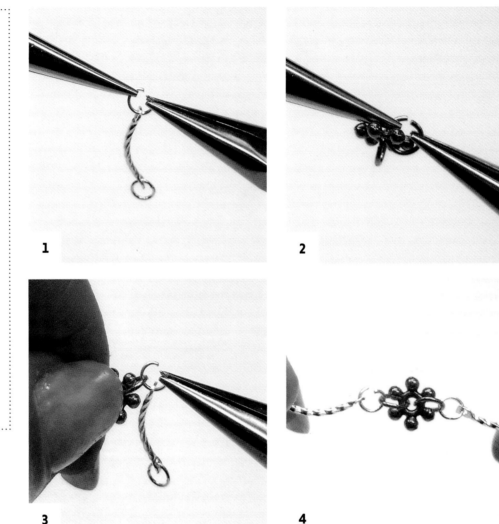

**1.** *Attach jump rings to the links.* Attach a silver jump ring to each end of all the silver links.

**2.** *Attach jump rings to the daisies.* Attach two 5mm gold jump rings to ten daisy spacers.

**3.** *Attach the daisies and links together.* Open the jump ring at one end of a silver link and hook on one of the jump rings from a daisy spacer.

**4.** *Begin forming the daisy chains.* Attach another silver link to the other jump ring on the daisy spacer from Step 3. Make sure the inside curves of both links attached to the daisy spacer face the same way.

If you like a bold statement piece, this necklace might just suit your style. The daisy spacer and link chains at the front add some movement to an otherwise solid design.

7

**5. *Complete the first daisy chain.*** Continue connecting daisy spacers and links until you have a chain of five daisy spacers and six silver links.

**6. *Create the additional daisy chains.*** Create a second chain with four daisy spacers and three silver links. Then create a third chain with one daisy spacer and two silver links.

**7. *Attach jump rings.*** Attach a 6mm gold jump ring to each end of all three daisy chains.

**8. *String one end of the longest daisy chain.*** Remove the threaded ball from the neck wire and string on the 6mm jump ring at one end of the longest length of daisy chain. If stringing the chain on from left to right, make sure the inside curve of the links face left when they are in position. Reverse this if stringing from right to left.

8

9

10

11

**9. *String the medium daisy chain.***
String thirteen daisy spacers onto the wire. Then string on the jump ring at one end of the medium length of daisy chain, making sure the inside curve of the links face left if stringing from left to right.

**10. *String the shortest daisy chain.***
String nine daisy spacers onto the wire. Then string on the jump ring at one end of the shortest length of daisy chain, making sure the inside curve of the links face left if stringing from left to right.

**11. *String the tail of the shortest chain.*** String nineteen daisy spacers onto the wire. Then string on the jump ring at the other end of the shortest length of daisy chain.

**12. *Continue stringing the chains.***
String nine daisy spacers onto the wire. Then string on the jump ring at the other end of the medium length of daisy chain.

**13. *Complete the stringing.*** String thirteen daisy spacers onto the wire. Then string on the jump ring at the other end of the longest length of daisy chain. Return the threaded ball to the end of the neck wire.

# Clasps

Jewelry clasps come in many shapes and forms, but two of the more commonly used closures are spring-type clasps (like lobster claw clasps) and two-piece toggle and bar clasps. Study these clasps closely and you'll discover that they are more than just mechanical devices—they're also miniature masterpieces with sculptural qualities that can be used to great effect in jewelry making.

Who would have thought you could link lobster claw clasps together to create a fancy chain? Or that instead of performing their duty as a clasp, the two parts of a toggle could be used independently of each other as decorative elements? The jewelry in this section uses clasps in ways you may never have thought of, and you will be pleasantly surprised when you realize what you're looking at!

The designs in this section are innovative and just a bit cheeky—perfect for the rebel fashionista who likes to blur the boundaries between fashion and functionality. So I invite you to be a little daring too and wear your clasps front and center!

# Cha-Cha Ring

Finished size: 1⅜" (3.5cm) tall

### MATERIALS
- Thirty-eight 12mm gold lobster claw clasps
- Sixteen 4mm gold jump rings
- Gold 5-loop adjustable cha-cha ring base

### TOOLS
- Chain-nose pliers

**1**

**3**

**4**

**1. *Attach a jump ring.*** Open a jump ring and hook it through the small loop of a lobster claw clasp. Repeat with a second lobster claw clasp.

**2. *Prepare the sets of jump rings.*** Open a jump ring and hook the small loops of three lobster claw clasps onto it. Create ten of these in total.

**3. *Attach the single clasps.*** Attach the jump ring of one of the single lobster claw clasps to one of the outer loops of the ring base. Repeat with the remaining single lobster claw clasp and the other outer ring loop.

**4. *Begin attaching the three-clasp sets.*** Hook a jump ring through the second loop of the ring base and attach one three-clasp set onto each arm of the jump ring. Also hook on the loops of two additional clasps. Close the jump ring. This loop now has eight clasps in total attached to it.

**5. *Continue adding the clasps.*** Hook a jump ring through the center loop of the ring base and attach two three-clasp sets onto each arm of the jump ring (a total of twelve clasps). Also hook on the loops of two additional clasps. Close the jump ring.

**6. *Attach additional clasps to the center.*** Open a jump ring and hook on two three-clasp sets. Hook this jump ring onto the center loop of the ring base. The center loop now has twenty clasps in total attached to it.

**7. *Finish the ring.*** Repeat Step 4 on the fourth loop of the ring base.

This piece is super fun! All of the
attached clasps shimmer and shake,
creating sound and movement.

# Lobster Clasp Earrings

Finished length: 4½" (11.5cm)

**1. Create a set of copper clasps.** Open a 6mm jump ring and hook on the small loops of three copper lobster claw clasps, making sure the levers all face the same direction.

**2. Attach a jump ring to the silver clasp.** Attach a 4mm jump ring to the small loop of a silver lobster claw clasp.

**3. Create a chain of clasps.** Open a copper lobster claw clasp and hook it through the jump ring attached to the silver lobster claw clasp. Attach a 4mm jump ring to the small loop of the copper clasp. Repeat with a silver clasp to create a chain of three lobster claw clasps.

**4. Attach the earring wire.** Open the jump ring of the second silver clasp and hook it through the loop of an earring wire.

**5. Create a circular chain.** Separate the chain into two 9¼" (23.5cm) lengths. Set one aside for the second earring. Open the last link of the chain and hook on the first link of the chain to form a circle. Make sure the chain is not twisted before closing the link.

**6. Attach a clasp to the chain.** Open one of the outer clasps from the set of three created in Step 1 and hook it onto any link of the circular chain. Count over twenty-eight links and hook the other outer clasp onto this link.

**7. Hook the chain onto the center clasp.** Find the center link of the long loop of chain hanging down from the clasps. Hook this link onto the middle clasp of the three-clasp set.

**8**

**8. *Assemble the earring.*** Open the end silver lobster claw clasp from the chain of clasps in Step 3 and hook it onto the jump ring of the three copper clasps.

**9. *Make the second earring.***
Repeat Steps 1–8 to make a second matching earring.

Gold, silver, and copper come together for a mixed metal medley. You can make these earrings longer or shorter by adjusting the length of the chain pieces used, or by adding or removing clasps from the upper portion of the earrings.

# Antique Lobster Clasp and Toggle Necklace

Finished length: 18" (46cm)

## MATERIALS

- 28 antique copper lobster claw clasps
- 4 antique copper toggle and bar clasp sets
- Three 3mm antique copper jump rings
- Thirty-three 4mm antique copper jump rings
- One 6mm antique copper jump ring
- 9⅝" (25cm) of 5 x 3.5mm antique copper oval link chain

## TOOLS

- Chain-nose pliers

**1**

**2**

**1. Create a chain of clasps.** Open a 4mm jump ring and hook on the small loop of a lobster claw clasp. Open a second lobster claw clasp and hook it onto the jump ring, making sure the levers of both clasps face the same way. Open a jump ring and hook it through the small loop of the clasp just added. Continue adding clasps and jump rings until you have a chain of six clasps and six jump rings.

**2. Add another clasp.** Hook the small loop of another lobster claw clasp onto the last jump ring of the chain from Step 1. The loop of the clasp should face the opposite direction of the others in the chain, but the lever should still face the same way.

**3. Add another clasp.** Open the first lobster claw clasp in the chain and hook on a 4mm jump ring. Open another lobster claw clasp and hook it onto the jump ring you added. This clasp should face the opposite direction of the first clasp in the chain, but the levers should still face the same way. You should now have a chain of eight clasps, with the first and last clasp facing one direction and the remaining clasps facing the opposite direction.

**4. Create the other side of the necklace.** Repeat Steps 1–3 to create a matching chain of clasps. Open a 4mm jump ring and hook on the small loop of the eighth clasp of each chain.

**5. Prepare the connector clasps.** Open a lobster claw clasp and hook on a jump ring. Repeat nine times for a total of ten.

If you like the look of antiqued metal, this piece is perfect for you. But if you prefer the look of gold or silver, simply use findings in those colors instead.

**6**

**7**

**8**

**9**

**6. Attach pairs of clasps to the necklace.** Counting from the left end of the chain, attach the jump rings of the clasps from Step 5 to the following clasps of the chain: second, third, fifth, sixth, eighth, ninth, eleventh, twelfth, fourteenth, and fifteenth. The lever of the first clasp attached should face left, the lever of the second clasp should face right, and so on.

**7. Connect the pairs of clasps together.** Use 4mm jump rings to connect the small loops of all but the center pair of clasps just added to the chain.

**8. Connect the center pair of clasps together.** Use a 3mm jump ring to connect the center pair of clasps. Then attach a 3mm jump ring to the small loop of each center clasp. Hook the small loop of a lobster claw clasp onto each of these jump rings. The center pair of clasps should now be connected with two additional clasps suspended from them.

**9. Attach the decorative elements.** Starting with the left pair of clasps suspended from the chain, attach a 4mm jump ring to the jump ring connecting the clasps. Before closing the jump ring, hook on the ring half of a toggle clasp. Repeat with the remaining pairs of clasps, attaching toggle rings to the odd pairs and toggle bars to the even pairs, using the 6mm jump ring to connect the center pair to a toggle ring. You will have one toggle bar left over. Set this aside for another project.

**10. Attach the chains.** Separate the chain into two equal lengths and attach one length to each end of the necklace.

**11. Attach the clasp.** Open the last chain link at each end of the necklace and add one half of the toggle and bar clasp to each side.

# Scalloped Chain Necklace

Finished length: 17¼" (44cm)

## MATERIALS

- Sixty-six 12mm silver lobster claw clasps
- Five 25 x 8mm silver 3-hole spacers
- Seventy-eight 6mm silver jump rings
- Fifteen silver eye pins
- Silver toggle and bar clasp

## TOOLS

- Chain-nose pliers
- Round-nose pliers
- Flush cutters

This elegant necklace will add an extra special touch to any outfit you wear for a sophisticated evening out.

**1. _Prepare the spacers._** Thread eye pins through the three holes of a spacer and turn a simple loop at the end of each one. Repeat for all the spacers.

**2. _Prepare the lobster claw clasps._** Attach a jump ring to the small loop of every lobster claw clasp.

**3. _Create the short links._** Take two lobster claw clasps. Open one and hook it onto the jump ring of the other. Make sure the levers of both clasps face the same way. Repeat to make six short links in total.

**4. _Create the clasp chains._** Following the method in Step 3, make six chains with three clasps, four chains with four clasps, and four chains with five clasps. Set two of the three-clasp chains aside for Step 10.

**5. _Attach the chains to the spacer bars._** Open the end jump ring of one of the three-clasp chains and attach it to the top eye pin loop on the right side of a spacer bar. Attach a jump ring to the top eye pin loop on the left side of the spacer. Open the end clasp of one of the three-clasp chains and attach it to the jump ring you just added. The clasps of both chains should face the same direction, as should their levers.

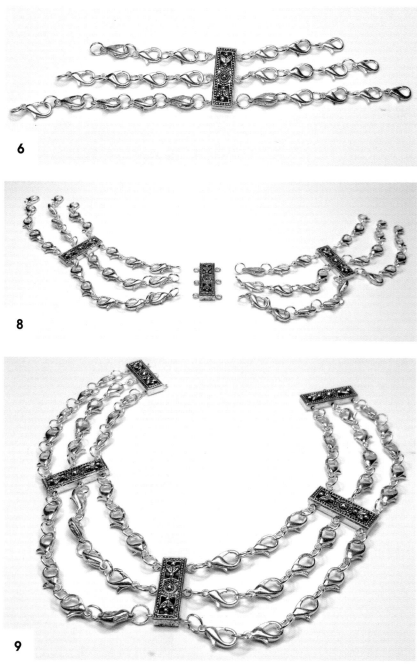

**6**

**8**

**9**

**10**

**6. Continue attaching the chains.** Repeat Step 5 to attach the four-clasp chains to the middle eye pin loops. Then attach the five-clasp chains to the bottom eye pin loops.

**7. Create another spacer bar with chains.** Repeat Steps 5 and 6 to create another spacer component, but with the clasps facing opposite directions so the two components mirror each other.

**8. Connect the two halves of the necklace.** Lay out the two spacer components side by side with the clasps of the two components facing opposite directions. Place a spacer between the two components and connect one end of each component to it in the center using the jump rings and eye pin loops.

**9. Attach the end spacer bars.** Attach a spacer bar to each end of the necklace.

**10. Attach the side chains and gather them.** Working on the left side of the necklace, attach the end jump ring of a two-clasp chain to each of the eye pin loops of the end spacer bar. Then, hook the end clasp of each of these chains onto the end jump ring of one of the three-clasp chains set aside in Step 4. Repeat on the right side of the necklace.

**11. Attach the clasp.** Attach one half of the clasp to each end of the necklace.

# Hollow Tubes

Hollow tubes, or noodle beads as they are also known, are sleek, modern jewelry findings that lend a fashionable elegance to your jewelry. Including a few hollow tubes in a project will add graceful, flowing lines that draw your eye all around the design. But build an entire design with hollow tubes and you'll have a piece with real *wow* factor!

These classy components—sometimes patterned, sometimes curved, and sometimes straight—can be strung onto both rigid and flexible stringing materials, making them suitable for a variety of styles. Release your inner urban warrior and make a bold design statement with a tribal-inspired choker. Or show your logical side and construct a geometric bracelet with vertical and diagonal lines. Or create something as delicate as the light and airy Butterfly Petal ring (page 93). There are so many looks you can achieve with these versatile tubes—you're bound to find something in a style that suits you.

# Tubular Bells   Finished length: 2⅞" (7.5cm)

## MATERIALS

- Ten 30 x 1.5mm gold twisted hollow tubes
- Eight 20 x 1.5mm silver twisted hollow tubes
- Two 5 x 7mm silver filigree basket bead caps
- Eighteen 41mm silver head pins
- 2 silver eye pins
- 12" (30.5cm) of 2 x 3mm silver oval chain
- 2 silver earring wires

## TOOLS

- Round-nose pliers
- Chain-nose pliers
- Flush cutters

1

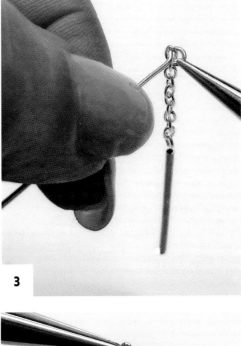

3

4

**1. *Prepare the hollow tubes.*** Thread half of the gold and half of the silver hollow tubes onto head pins and create a simple loop (see page 9) at the end of each one.

**2. *Separate the chain.*** Separate the silver chain into two equal lengths and set one piece aside for the second earring. Separate the remaining piece into the following lengths: one 1" (2.5cm); four ¾" (2cm); one 9/16" (1.4cm); two ⅜" (1cm); and one 9/32" (0.7cm).

**3. *Place the center tube in position.*** Open the loop of a gold tube head pin and attach it to the end of the 1" (2.5cm) chain. Attach an eye pin to the other end of the chain. String the filigree bead cap onto the eye pin through the center hole. Then, create a wrapped loop (see page 10) after the bead cap to hold it in place.

**4. *Attach the chains to the edge of the bead cap.*** Open the last link of each of the remaining chain pieces and hook them onto the holes around the outside of the filigree bead cap, alternating short and long lengths around the bead cap.

**5. *Attach the tubes.*** Open the loop of one of the gold tube head pins and attach it to the shortest chain. Attach the remaining tubes to the chain ends, alternating gold and silver tubes.

**6. *Attach the earring wire.*** Open the loop of the earring wire and hook on the wrapped loop.

**7. *Make the second earring.*** Repeat Steps 1–6 to make a second matching earring.

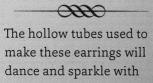

The hollow tubes used to make these earrings will dance and sparkle with your every movement.

# Spiral Orb Earrings

Finished length: 4½" (11.5cm)

## MATERIALS

- Twelve 25 x 2mm gold hollow spiral noodle tubes
- Six 3mm gold spacer beads
- Two 5 x 3mm gold spacer beads
- Two 8mm gold filigree beads
- Two 6mm gold filigree beads
- Two 3mm gold filigree beads
- 8 gold crimp covers
- 6 size 2 gold crimp tubes
- 2 size 3 gold crimp tubes
- 24" (61cm) of 0.015" gold beading wire
- 2 gold earring wires

## TOOLS

- Regular crimping pliers
- Large crimping pliers
- Chain-nose pliers
- Flush cutters

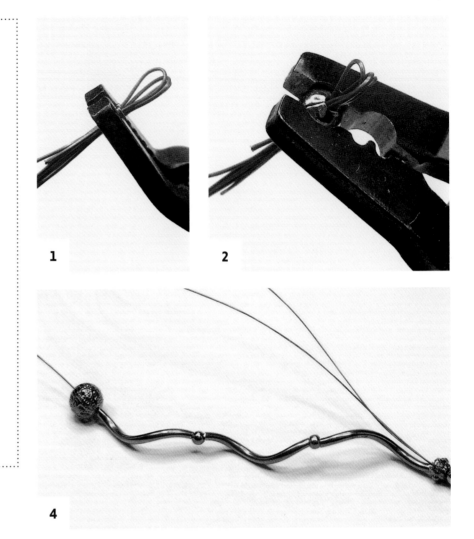

**1**

**2**

**4**

**1. Prepare the beading wire.** Cut the beading wire in half and set one piece aside for the second earring. Cut the other piece into three lengths measuring 9" (23cm), 8" (20cm), and 7" (18cm). Even up the ends of the three wire pieces and string a size 3 crimp tube onto them. Bring the wire ends back through the crimp, forming a small loop, and crimp them securely.

**2. Cover the crimp tube.** Place a crimp cover over the crimp tube, enclosing it completely. Using the large crimping pliers, gently and evenly close the cover so the seam is invisible.

**3. String a spacer bead.** String a spacer bead onto all three strands of wire and trim the short ends close to the bead.

**4. String the longest wire.** String three hollow tubes, with a 3mm spacer bead between each one, onto the longest wire. Then string on an 8mm filigree bead.

These stunning earrings are accented by the filigree beads and wire loops at the base of each strand.

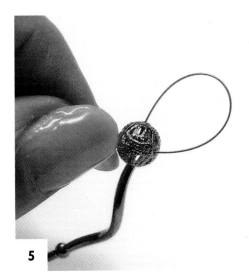

**5**

**5. Create loops on the filigree bead.** Thread the wire in and out of the filigree bead a few times, creating three or four loops. Do not pull the wire tight against the bead, but leave it loose so the loops stand out from the bead.

**6. Feed the wire back into the bead.** Bring the wire out through the hole in the filigree bead. String a size 2 crimp onto the wire, pushing it up against the filigree bead. Bring the end of the wire back through the crimp tube, the bead, and the first hollow tube, leaving a small loop at the end. Crimp securely.

**7. Finish the end.** Trim away the loop just formed at the bottom of the wire. Place a crimp cover over the crimp and enclose it as in Step 2.

**8. String the medium and short wires.** Repeat Steps 4–7 with the medium length of beading wire, using two hollow tubes, one spacer bead, and a 6mm filigree bead. Then repeat Steps 4–7 with the shortest length using one hollow tube and a 3mm filigree bead.

**9. Attach the earring wire.** Open the loop of an earring wire and hook on the wire loop at the top of the earring.

**10. Make the second earring.** Repeat Steps 1–9 to make a second matching earring.

**6**

**7**

# Fan Wave Bracelet

Finished size: 2½" (6.5cm) internal diameter

## MATERIALS

- Twenty-four 30 x 2mm silver twisted hollow tubes
- Twenty-four 14 x 2mm copper twisted hollow tubes
- Twenty-four 41mm silver eye pins
- 24" (61cm) of 1mm beading elastic

## TOOLS

- Scissors
- Chain-nose pliers
- Round-nose pliers
- Flush cutters
- 2 bead stoppers
- Jewelry adhesive (I used G-S Hypo Cement)

This fun geometric design might just become your favorite everyday piece, but don't be afraid to pair it with formal outfits as well!

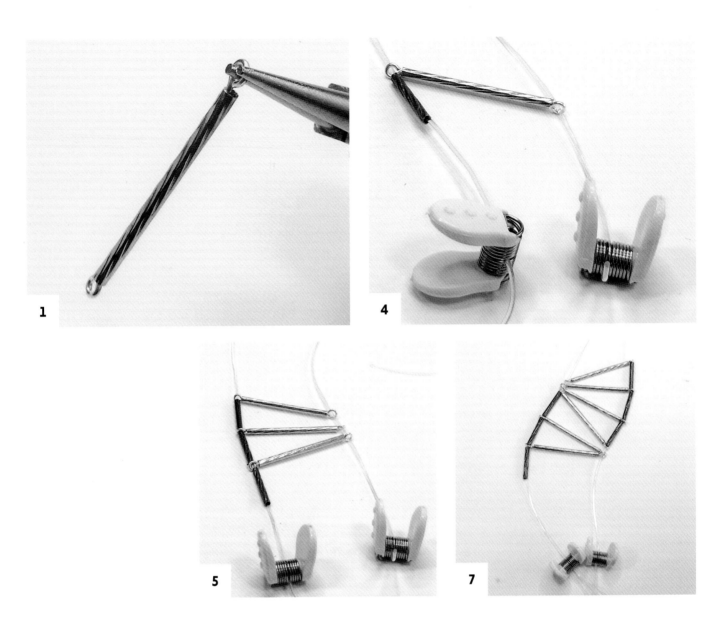

**1. Prepare the silver tubes.** Thread each silver tube onto an eye pin and turn a simple loop (see page 9) at the end.

**2. Prepare the beading elastic.** Prepare the beading elastic by stretching it several times. Then cut it into two 12" (30.5cm) lengths. Place a bead stopper at one end of each length.

**3. Position the project on your workspace.** Position the two elastic cords parallel to one another on your workspace with the bead stoppers closest to you and the loose ends toward the top.

**4. String the first two tubes.** String a copper tube on the left cord. Thread the left cord through the loop of a silver tube eye pin. Thread the right cord through the other loop of the same eye pin.

**5. Complete the first half of the stringing pattern.** Repeat Step 4 twice more so you have a total of three copper tubes and three silver tube eye pins strung onto the elastic cords.

**6. Begin the second half of the stringing pattern.** String a copper tube onto the right hand cord. Thread the left cord through the loop of a silver tube eye pin. Thread the right cord through the other loop of the same eye pin.

**7. Complete the second half of the stringing pattern.** Repeat Step 6 twice more so you have a total of three copper tubes strung onto the right cord, alternating with three silver tube eye pins.

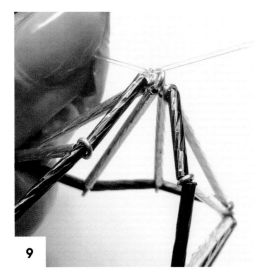

**8. *Continue stringing the bracelet.*** Continue this stringing pattern until all the tubes have been strung.

**9. *Finish the bracelet.*** Remove the bead stoppers. Tie two opposing cords from each end of the bracelet together in a half knot. Tie a second knot and pull all strands of the elastic to tighten and secure it. Repeat with the remaining two cord ends. Dab jewelry adhesive onto the knots and allow it to dry. Thread the cord ends back into the nearest hollow tube and then trim away the excess cord.

# Tribal Tube Choker

Finished size: 5½" (14cm) internal diameter

## MATERIALS

- Five 30 x 4mm curved hollow silver tubes (3mm inner diameter)
- Eighteen 20 x 2mm curved hollow silver tubes
- Eighteen 25 x 2mm curved hollow gunmetal tubes
- Sixty-four 6mm silver daisy spacers (with 1.5mm holes)
- Twenty 2mm silver spacer beads
- Forty-eight 3mm silver spacer beads
- Thirty-six 40mm silver head pins
- Four 50mm silver head pins
- One 61mm silver head pin
- 16" (40.5cm) 1mm silver neck wire with threaded ball screw

## TOOLS

- Flat-nose pliers
- Round-nose pliers
- Flush cutters
- Regular crimping pliers
- Large crimping pliers
- ½" (1.5cm) mandrel to curve the head pins around (I used the handle of a needle tool)

**1**

**2**

**4**

**1. *Prepare the tubes.*** Using the flush cutters, trim two 4mm diameter silver tubes to 1" (2.5cm) long. Trim six 2mm diameter gunmetal tubes to ¾" (2cm) long and two gunmetal tubes to ⅝" (1.5cm) long. Trim six 2mm diameter silver tubes to ⅝" (1.5cm) long and two silver tubes to ⅜" (1cm) long. Use the large crimping pliers to reshape the cut ends of the 4mm tubes and the regular crimping tubes to reshape the 2mm tubes.

**2. *Curve the bottom section of each head pin.*** Shape the bottom ¾" (2cm) of each of the 40mm head pins by bending them around the mandrel.

**3. *String all the 2mm diameter tubes.*** Thread all the gunmetal tubes onto curved head pins. On each of the remaining curved head pins, string a 2mm spacer bead and a 2mm diameter silver tube.

**4. *Turn simple loops on all the head pins.*** Working on one curved head pin at a time, hold it between your thumb and index finger with the inside curve facing to the left. Using the flat-nose pliers, bend the tail of the head pin toward the back, close to the top of the tube. Trim the head pin 9⁄32" (0.5cm) from the bend. Turn a small simple loop (see page 9) using the very tip of the jaws of the round-nose pliers. Repeat for all the head pins.

**5. *String the longest 4mm diameter tube and turn a simple loop.*** On the 61mm head pin, string a 2mm spacer bead, a 3mm spacer bead, a daisy spacer, and a 4mm diameter tube. String 3mm spacer beads onto the head pin to fill the tube. Add a daisy spacer, a 3mm spacer bead, and a 2mm spacer bead. Turn a small simple loop (see page 9) at the end of the head pin.

With a mix of gunmetal and silver tubes, this stunning choker combines tribal and industrial style.

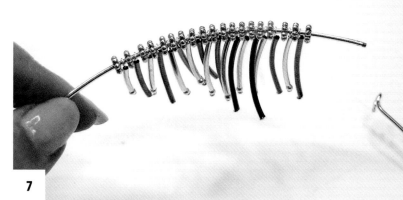

**7**

**9**

**6. *Prepare the remaining 4mm diameter tubes.*** On the 50mm head pins, thread a daisy spacer and a 4mm diameter tube. Fill the tube with 3mm spacer beads and then add a daisy spacer. Turn small simple loops (see page 9) at the end of each head pin.

**7. *Begin stringing the necklace.*** Unscrew the threaded ball from the end of the neck wire and set it aside. Thread on a daisy spacer. Then, string on the head pin tubes, alternating between silver and gunmetal, placing a daisy spacer between each one. Start with a ⅜" (1cm) silver tube, ⅝" (1.5cm) gunmetal tube, ⅝" (1.5cm) silver tube, and a ¾" (2cm) gunmetal tube, followed by a daisy spacer. String two more of each of the ⅝" (1.5cm) silver tubes and ¾" (2cm) gunmetal tubes, alternating colors and stringing a daisy spacer between each one.

**8. *Continue stringing the necklace.*** Continue with the stringing pattern by stringing five ¾" (2cm) silver tubes and five 1" (2.5cm) gunmetal tubes, alternating colors and stringing a daisy spacer between each one.

**9. *String the center of the necklace.*** For the center of the necklace, string on three daisy spacers, the shortest 4mm diameter tube, three daisy spacers, the medium 4mm diameter tube, three daisy spacers, and the longest 4mm diameter tube.

**10. *Finish stringing the necklace.*** String the other half of the necklace in reverse order to match the first half. Center all the components and screw the threaded ball back onto the end of the neck wire.

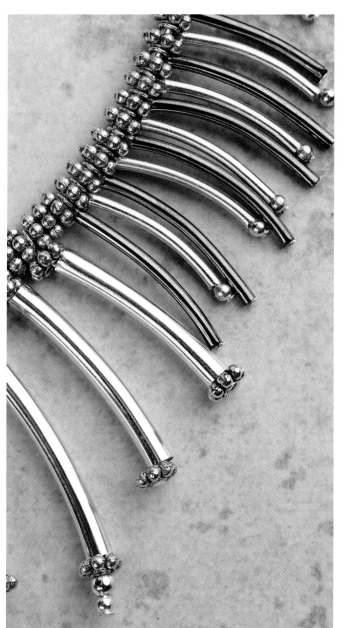

# Butterfly Petal Ring

Finished size: 1¼" (3cm) diameter

## MATERIALS

- Eight 11 x 1mm curved liquid silver hollow tubes
- Twenty-five 8.5 x 1mm curved liquid silver hollow tubes
- Fourteen 6 x 1mm straight liquid silver hollow tubes
- 1 silver adjustable filigree ring
- 28-gauge non-tarnish silver wire

## TOOLS

- Flat-nose pliers
- Flush cutters
- Nylon jaw pliers

This piece is the perfect summertime accessory. Pair it with a white dress or your favorite flowing skirt.

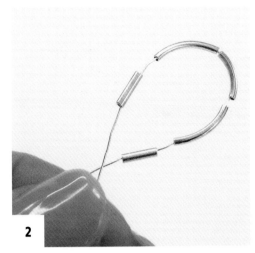

**2**

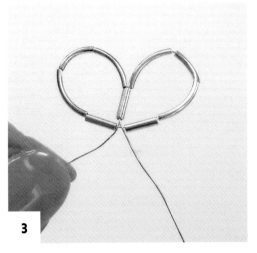

**3**

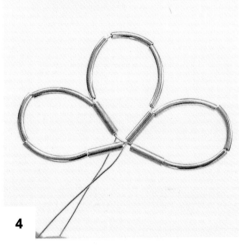

**4**

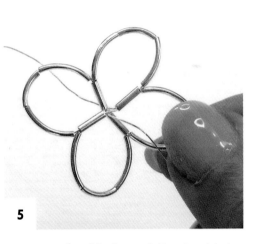

**5**

**1. *Cut the wire.*** Cut a 32" (81cm) length of wire.

**2. *Form the first petal.*** Leave a 6" (15cm) tail on the wire and string on a straight tube, a long curved tube, a short curved tube, a long curved tube, and a straight tube. Form them into a petal shape by looping the wire.

**3. *Create the second petal.*** String a straight tube, a long curved tube, a short curved tube, and a long curved tube onto the wire. Then thread the wire back through the first straight tube of the first petal. The will form the second petal, with the two petals sharing a straight tube.

**4. *Create the third petal.*** For the third petal, string a straight tube, a long curved tube, a short curved tube, and a long curved tube onto the wire. Then thread the wire back through the first straight tube of the second petal.

**5. *Create the fourth petal.*** For the fourth petal, thread the wire through the straight tube of the first petal that is not connected to the second petal. String a long curved tube, a short curved tube, and a long curved tube onto the wire. Then thread the wire through the straight tube of the third petal that is not connected to the second petal. You now have four petals in all.

**Tip**
The wire will get crinkled as you work with it. Always take your time when threading it through the tubes and make sure to untwist it so it does not kink as you pull it through. To make it easier to thread the wire through the tubes, run the wire through the nylon jaw pliers to restraighten it as needed.

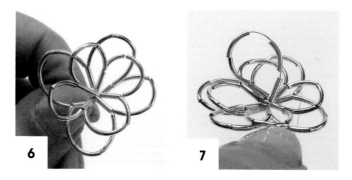

6

7

**6. Create the middle layer of petals.** Continue making petals by repeating Steps 2–5, substituting short curved tubes for the long curved tubes. Bind the middle layer to the bottom layer by wrapping the wire around and between the petals. Bring the wire back up to the top.

**7. Create the inner layer of petals.** String a straight tube, three small curved tubes, and a straight tube onto the wire. Wrap the wire from the top of the flower down to the base of the flower and back up to the top twice to secure the petal in place. Repeat to create two more inner petals in the same way.

**8. Position the flower on the ring.** Place the flower over the center of the filigree ring base and insert the wire ends through two adjacent holes.

**9. Wire the flower to the ring.** Wrap the wire around the ring shank and pass it back to the top, in between the loops of the petals. Repeat several times until the flower is secure. Finish with the two wire ends at the top.

**10. Trim the wire.** Working with one wire end at a time, insert it into one of the straight tubes and pull it through with pliers. Insert it into the adjacent curved tube, pull it through, and then trim away the excess, taking care not to cut the wire passing through the tubes that form the petals. Repeat with the second wire end.

**11. Position the petals.** Manipulate the petals into a flower shape.

### Tip

The inner petals are created individually without passing the wire through the straight tubes of the adjacent petals. As you make each one, wrap the wire once around the bottom two layers of petals to secure it.

8

9

10

# Sources and Acknowledgments

Many of the jewelry findings used in this book can be sourced from your local bead shop or craft store. I used products from the following companies when making the projects for this book. Please feel free to select the materials and products you like and that work best for you as you create your own jewelry findings projects.

All About Beads www.allaboutbeads.com.au, findings), Beadalon (www.beadalon.com), Eastern Findings Corp (www.easternfindings.com, findings), Feeling Inspired (www.feelinginspired.com.au, chain and findings), Fire Mountain Gems and Beads (www.firemountaingems.com, findings).

# Index